OMG! MY FIRST DAY

"Today is the first day of the rest of your life."

APRIL L. THOMAS, MSW

ISBN-13: 978-0-578-51986-9

DEDICATION

I would like to first give honor and thanks to my Lord and Savior Jesus Christ. My husband Christopher, my children Ebonie and Elijah, my family and dearest close friends, whom have been there for me and have been a blessing throughout my life's journey. I am especially grateful for your unconditional love; continue support and inspiration in pursing my dreams and future endeavors.

ACKNOWLEDGEMENTS

A special thanks and appreciation, to those whom supported the vision, imagination and creation of this book project.

Regina Peacock

Krista M. Messam

Dominique E. Jones

Ti'Aira K. Perdue

Doresa Henderson

CONTENTS

INTRODUCTION

Imagine, who would have ever thought that the very first life experiences are the first steps taken, they shape us into who we are in the present and whom we will become in the future. This book presents a variety of meaningful first time experiences through the life span of early and late adulthood.

I.
A NEW DAY: TAKING THE FIRST STEPS

———◆———◇———◆———

"Today is the first day of the rest of your life." - American Proverb. The majority of people fail to remember that a new beginning starts the very second one starts breathing. With this awareness of inspiration and imagination filled with possibilities, you can feel positively buoyant. While you do not know what you will create the next second, you can examine all the potential opportunities that lay before you to determine what suits you best. When you choose to direct your energy toward the opportunities that are best for you, the universe supports you, while also contributing to the collective unconscious wisdom.

By choosing your preferences from all the possibilities available to you, you learn more about the life you will create, and then actually begin to co-create it with the universe. Yes, that is right. Co-create it with the universe, i.e., Law of Attraction and Law of Abundance.

Even the buoyancy you feel as you recognize all the potential opportunities that lay before you, you are drawing the situation to you with the best energetic match. Part of recognizing what you want is the ability to discern when something is not right for you, thus, all your energy can be directed toward bringing the things you desire into form. When the universe sends its assistance, you will feel as if you are floating toward your dreams upon a swift breeze. When you experience the universe working with you, co-creating your world through you and around you, all the opportunities that arise become proof of your creative abilities. You can truly enjoy and look forward to the manifestations of your desires and dreams.

"Be optimistic, let go of your fears, and have faith, because you will never know if you will be successful unless you try."
- April L. Thomas, MSW

II.
A NEW MILESTONE: YOUTH TO ADULTHOOD

Transmiting from youth to adulthood and self-reliance can be challenging for any young person. So why should any young person listen to an older one about the best way to become a grown-up?

Well, there is a part of the brain which does not fully develop in most of us until the age of twenty-four years old and is accountable for regulating mood, controlling impulses, attention span, and the capacity to plan ahead as well as understand the consequences of a person's actions.

Meanwhile, it is up to adults to guide them by showing them possible consequences, good and bad, of their behavior.

You have to grow fast and transit even more quickly if you want to make it.

With that in mind, let's look at some useful habits I believe is the transition from youth to adulthood:

> ### *Who You Are as an Individual*

The most significant and problematic challenge of transiting into adulthood is to figure out who you are, what you care about, believe in, and stand for because we are all raised with people telling us what to think, how to act, and what to say.

These people are usually parents, teachers, friends, and other so-called authorities. Most of the times, when given a choice, young people, as well as adults, seek the easiest path, the path of least resistance, just so they can be accepted.

But it is in those moments when you opt for a different route that it can define you as an individual. The important thing is to make those decisions for yourself, not because of authority figures or out of fear of losing someone's affection, but out of the conviction of who you are and who you want to be.

> ### *Fight the Fear of the Unknown*

Whether it comes in the form of different ideas, different cultures, or different food, we all have an inclination to dislike what we do not understand because of fear of the unknown.

People's brains who do reject new experience do release an addictive chemical that makes them feel better. In that way, your body is encouraging your ignorance and fear. You need to fight such impulse. Becoming an adult means growing, learning, understanding and not shying away into a comfort zone.

But remember not to confuse intellectual bravery with physical courage. It is harder to change your mind about an opinion than it is to jump out of a plane. Exploring a new culture or examining a new idea will make you grow and make you the kind of person others will be interested in.

> ### *Stand Up for What You Believe in*

It is not enough to have high ideals and beliefs; you sometimes have to get off the couch and stand up for those beliefs. This is especially hard when you are hanging with your friends, and they all express an opinion that is the opposite of yours.

Because you are outnumbered, it is easy for them to ridicule your opinion. Stand firm, defend your views and beliefs, be an adult version of yourself. More importantly, you will feel proud that you took a stand because doing nothing will hunt you for a long time.

> ### *Talk and Action*

You have to realize that there is one main difference between a young person and an adult. Young people talk about what they want to do while real adults act and put those things into action. The second difference is that adults are more organized because they have less time to do more.

Successful adults make a to-do list, and they do not put off doing things until later. They know that being organized can change your life. You should focus on priorities which need to be done now; you do things you need to finish and don't say "I'll do it tomorrow," which in turn makes you much more successful.

➢ *Pay Attention to Advice and Guidance*

Understand that whatever difficulties and doubts you are facing in your youth, millions of people before you have gone through the same experience. Paying attention to people's advice and guidance does not always mean you should take it, but you can make a decision as to which advice is right for you.

To transit from youth to adulthood, it is also a good idea to gather some books and biographies of successful people who came before you, so you can refer to them when you need to.

If you do not learn from the experiences of others and yourself, you will end up making the same mistakes over and over. Therefore, when somebody gives you advice, do not dismiss it just because they are older.

➢ *Get Mentors to Copy*

Many successful adults are worthwhile looking up to, even to following and copying. The world is full of them but you need to pick the right people for the right reasons.

Skip celebrities who make a lot of money, act stupidly and unwisely. They chase fame and glory so obsessively, they are not interested in anything else and have no desire to learn.

Do not make the mistake of believing that just because these people can act or sing, all of them also have valuable insights into wisdom or culture. Instead, find successful adults that represent the values that you want to have, and not the fame they have.

➢ *Choose the Right Friends*

When you grow up and transit to adulthood, it is good friends who are helping you through the tough parts of life. Bad friends, on the other hand, would often be the cause of most of your problems.

So, do not befriend young people just to get back at someone or to try to be something that you are not. You would waste that way a lot of your youth and miss out of some great friendships.

➤ *Beware of Your Manners*

When you are a young person, being told to keep your elbows off the table, firmly shake hands, respect people or ask someone if they would like something to drink, it all seems like a lot of illogical rules.

Know that part of transiting from youth to adulthood is the awareness that it does not matter whether or not the rules of manners make sense. What is important is the effect of following these rules and that people do appreciate them which in turn gives you respect.

➤ *Be Autonomous*

An actual adult can take care of himself and his day-to-day needs. Learn to make your bed, pass the vacuum, do your laundry, cook, or even manually fix things.

The sooner you begin doing things by yourself, the sooner you get respect and feel proud, and enriched.

➤ *Never Act on "I Dare You"*

I believe that the three very unsafe words for young people are, "I dare you." The challenge to prove "you can" to others is very tempting, especially since they might believe that you don't have what it takes.

They may call you 'chicken' but know that by refusing a dare you display more intelligence, courage, and independence than anyone who makes the challenge thinking they are brave. I call it stupidity.

➤ *Do Not Be Afraid of Your Adult Version*

While transitting from youth to adulthood, priorities will shift, and friends will change. It may be scary for most young people to become an adult by following all of the above suggestions. And surely when the example you have is shouting orders or barking by saying "When I was your age... "

Do not worry, be yourself, know who you are, what you stand for, watch for any attacks on your principles, but always be open to change if an indication comes up.

Finally, most of what is important to you now won't be in a few years. Avoid doing permanent things that someday you may regret because your taste in styles, music, type of girls or boys, your thoughts, and even pretty much everything will change.

III.
GOING TO COLLEGE: FIRST YEAR STUDENT

After your parents have dropped you off at college and have headed back home, you may experience a slight shutter of apprehension. However, you will get off on the right foot and feel more comfortable with this new and important experience, if you pay close attention to and act on the eight suggestions that follow.

Make Friends - Smile! Be Friendly! Talk to everyone. Do things in groups. Include everyone anytime you go somewhere or do something. Accept people who are different from you. Try to understand the differences. Look for the best in others. The more friends you make in the early days of college, the easier the transition will be.

➤ *Explore the Campus*

As a group, walk around campus and around town. Find out where everything is located. Learn about the various campus departments, interesting locations (the library, the gym, and the pool), activities, organizations and potential employment opportunities. Go to town with a few friends. Check out the shopping, theater and recreational opportunities. In the early going, get out of your dorm. Make a point of going to a variety of campus and community events and activities. Laugh! Have some fun.

➤ *Search for a Direction*

Check out the fields that already hold some interest for you. Recognize that it is important to select a field of study where you will enjoy the work, one that is in line with your talents and skills. Do some research. Talk to others about your options and

11

opportunities. You can talk with upper class students, alumni, career counselors, employers or faculty advisors and staff members.

➤ *Keep Your Grades Up*

As you move through your freshman year, it is important to keep up with your grades. Be willing to put in the time, effort and actions necessary to achieve good grades. Since it is easy to stray toward a less demanding path, it takes much discipline to avoid the pitfalls of college life.

➤ *Deal with Your Fears*

Everyone has fears. You may fear failure, speaking in public, voicing your opinions in class, taking on a leadership role, meeting new people, joining a club or a million other things. Take some small risks, so you can try a few new things. Only by occasionally getting out of your comfort zone can you begin to grow and expand your possibilities for the future. Only a few people, if any, have achieved great things by staying in their comfort zone 100% of the time. The only way to deal with your fears is to take action, change your behavior and move in a new direction.

➤ *Develop a Healthy Curiosity*

Curious people are those who learn and grow. They read, research, ask questions, closely observe, experiment, learn from others and regularly try new things. A healthy curiosity is essential for success. College is the ideal place for students to begin to discover and become who they really are.

➤ *Operate with a Positive Attitude*

The attitude you present to the world, tell others who and what you are. Since we all need other people to help us move toward success, it is extremely important for students to present a friendly, upbeat, helpful attitude to the outside world. When that happens, others will be attracted to these positive words, behaviors, and traits.

➤ *Develop Your Plan of Action*

Once you select a direction, create a written plan, and lay out the steps that will lead you to your goal (a great job or acceptance to graduate school). The odds for success are greatly increased when you clearly understand what and how much has to be. As you move up the ladder of success, you will find that it is highly unlikely that you can regularly achieve your most important goals by winging it.

Most of the time, success is a choice that you make. Since you have the ability to succeed in college and beyond, these recommendations can help to ensure that you begin your college experience with the right approach. When you follow a few sensible suggestions and keep an eye toward your educational and career goals, you will find that your college experience is positive, fun and rewarding.

IV.
PREPARING YOUR CHILD: THE FIRST DAY OF PRESCHOOL

The first day of school for a child can be full of excitement as well as anxiety for both you and your child. Here are a few tips to help make the transition a smoother one.

➤ Read Books About Preschool

Read some books together about going to preschool and discuss the pictures. Talk about where they might sit or activities they might do such as painting.

➤ Schedule a Visit

Schedule a visit to the school to get your child familiar with the room and point out where they will play, have lunch and sit for a story. Show them where they will put their belongings if there are cubby holes. If it is allowed, take a few pictures to share and review when you get home. Making a book with the pictures can be a fun way to familiarize your child with their new school.

➤ Shop for Supplies

Let your child help pick out their supplies at the store. Getting a new outfit, a pair of shoes or a neat lunchbox for school also is another way to help get your child excited about the first day.

➤ Practicing

Let your child practice opening their pencil boxes and putting their supplies inside. Have your child practice putting their crayons back in the box and closing their glue stick caps. Closing marker caps and practicing how to hold a scissors properly are also skills that will be helpful to your child and his/her teacher.

Although tedious, labeling each crayon, scissors, and glue is very helpful for your child to keep track of their belongings as well as reinforcing name recognition.

> ### *Lunchboxes and Containers*

When you select your lunch containers, find ones your child can recognize and be sure to label them with their name. Have your child practice opening them. Many containers will be difficult at first, but they will learn quickly. If you have separate containers for their sandwich or fruit, show them which one will hold what part of their lunch.

> ### *Explain the Daily Routine*

If you can get a daily schedule, you can explain to your child what events will occur each day such as snack time, sharing, recess and pick up time. Be sure to explain that you will be dropping them off and picking them up. Sometimes letting them know what you will be doing while they are in school such as grocery shopping helps them understand why you are leaving.

> ### *Tip*

The first couple days may require you to stay a few minutes at the beginning of class. But after your child has been in school for a few days, it is often better to leave them even if they are a little teary. Give them a big hug and reassure them that you will be back soon to pick them up. It can be hard seeing your child teary and anxious, but it is amazing how quickly children become excited about their first day at school.

> ### *Share their Day*

Talk about their day at school to show them how important it is to you and keep them excited about going the next day. Display pictures and things they make for the whole family to admire.

Preschool is a very special time for your child to begin enjoying their first school experiences and to start socializing with other children. Helping to prepare them for this special event can make their first school experience a successful one.

V.
FIRST TIME PARENTS: THE MAKING OF A GOOD PARENT

It is important to realize that you are not perfect. As you start raising a new born baby, mistakes are bound. Some major ones and some, monor. You must learn from these mistakes, and that is the important part. Keep repeating them and you will land in trouble.

As a couple, when they find out that they're going to be parents, panic strikes their hearts and they run to 'Parenting magazines' to seek help and guidance. Although this is a bona fide practice, it is not highly encouraged as the conflicting thoughts of various writers can create unwanted stress.

Before you rush to the bookstore to buy the latest edition of the most popular parenting magazines, reflect on the fact that nature did not hand us a manual for raising children, if it did, it would most probably have been a religion by now!

Good parents learn from the experiences they've had in their lives, and teach the lessons to their children. Parenting is a skill that is learnt over time, and the skills become refined with time.

Some of the characteristics of a good parent are as follows:

1. Being understanding

2. Being Considerate

3. Being kind

4. Being Patient

5. A good disciplinarian at the required times.

6. Being helpful

As you embark on this great journey of parenting, the tough tides of doubt will often assail you, and the unchartered waters of child raising will sometimes overwhelm you. At such times, the people to take advice from are your own parents. Yes, your own parents! In this regard, the following questions are relevant:

1. How was I raised by my parents?

2. Are my morals high?

3. Was I a happy child?

4. How did my parents discipline me?

5. How sensitive were my parents to my feelings etc.?

Some of the answers to the questions above will be negative in nature. How you deal with them is exactly what is going to make you a good parent. All the things that you were not happy about you can change. You can avoid making those mistakes.

Ultimately parenting is an organic process; it required the individual to be open minded and versatile. It is an all-day job, with no coffee breaks in between. When the pressure knob tightens, know that this is when you are being molded into a good parent. These tips will help you to sail in your journey of parenting. Happy sailing!

VI.
YOUR HEALTHY NEWBORN: FIRST DAY HOME

So, you came home with your baby. Whether it is your first-born or not, it's always an exhilarating experience and a opportunity to learn new things every day.

Your baby probably already had the first Hepatitis B vaccine and the newborn screen at the hospital. Also, he or she already passed the hearing test. Congratulations! This article reviews what you need to know about your newborn's developmental milestone, feedings, elimination, and safety.

There are some essential things to know when you bring your neonate home. First of all, per the hospital's recommendations, set up a follow-up appointment with your baby's health care provider (usually 3-4 days post-delivery). It is important to evaluate your infant, i.e., check weight, listen to the heart, etc. Also, you may have questions that need to be answered. Prepare a list before the visit, so that nothing gets forgotten! Most healthcare providers like when patients come to the appointment well prepared. It helps us address all of your needs!

This chapter reviews what you need to know.

➢ *Developmental Milestones*

Your baby should respond to noise. For example, she should startle at the sound of a slamming door or a barking dog. By the age of a month, your baby should be able to distinguish between the mom's voice and voices of other people. However, some babies have this ability from the very first days after birth. Your baby's vision is intact, but right now she can best see objects and faces placed 8-12 inches away from her face. Also, she does not like bright lights. Babies like to open their eyes in dim light by the adult standards.

> ### *Feedings*

During the first few weeks, don't worry about schedules: your baby should eat on demand, on average every 2-4 hours. However, babies experience rapid growth spurts from time to time, and during those times they may be hungry every 1-2 hours. Just play it by ear. Also, keep in mind that your baby's stomach is very small (about the size of her fist), so it can't hold more than a couple of ounces at the time. If you feed your infant formula and notice excessive spit ups, decrease the amount of the formula but feed your baby a little more often.

Don't let more than four hours pass between feedings. You do not want your baby get frustrated with hunger and make the feeding experience unpleasant. At any time, your breastfed or formula fed baby spits up excessively, talk to your health care provider. She may suggest a formula change or, on rare occasions, medication.

> ### *Elimination*

A healthy newborn should pass the first bowel movement (BM) within 36 hours after being born. After establishing a healthy BM pattern, your baby may go to the bathroom once or a few times a day, or every other day, or so. One thing to keep in minds is that not everybody has a BM every day! As long as your infant is comfortable between BMs and they do not look like pebbles, there is no reason for concern. Also, keep in mind that breast milk has much less waste than formula. Therefore, your baby may have less frequent and malodorous BMs than a formula-fed infant.

Urination is a good indication of hydration. A few days old baby should have at least 4-5 wet diapers and work her way up to more than 6 a day!

> ### *Safety*

The safest sleeping position for your baby is on her back. It decreases the chance of SIDS (Sudden Infant Death Syndrome). Co-sleeping of infants and parents is no longer recommended. Such sleeping arrangements create an unsafe environment for the baby who can suffocate on bedding or be crushed by a sleeping adult. Every baby should sleep in her own bassinet or crib. Smoking should not be allowed around your baby as well. Cigarette smoke exposure not only increases the risk of SIDS, but it also increases your baby's susceptibility to catching upper respiratory tract infections.

Practice measuring your baby's temperature. Should the temperature be 100F or above, undress the infant and let her cool off. Small babies overheat easily! After 15 minutes, check the temperature again. If the temperature is still 100F or above, your baby needs to be examined by a healthcare provider right away. That is true until the infant is 3-month-old, because until then the immune system does not know how to work efficiently and fever may be a sign of a serious illness.

VII.
MISTAKES TO AVOID: FIRST TIME PARENTS

As first-time parents, we want to make sure we do it right. We set rules and schedules, firmly abiding by them. With no other sibling to look to as role models, the first child looks up to his parents for examples. First-born children often walk and talk earlier than other birth orders. They have the desire to follow in their parents' footsteps and grow up being little adults.

There is nothing wrong in setting firm rules and routines for a child to follow. After all we just want the best for them. However, over-parenting and over-protecting your first-born can have adverse effects and strengthen the perfectionism in them. They grow up having high expectations of themselves, get frustrated when things do not go perfectly, and can eventually lose confidence in themselves.

Here are the top 5 mistakes any first-time parent wants to avoid to raise a happy, confident child.

➤ *Being an Improver*

When you set a task for your young child to do, for example, to make the bed, do not improve the task after the child has completed it. Avoid straightening out the wrinkles or smoothing that bump caused by a lost toy underneath the covers.

By doing so you are sending the signal to the child who thinks that, "I am not good enough." Learn to be flexible. Encourage and praise him when he has completed the task well enough. Be satisfied with a less-than-perfect job.

Let it go, shut the door, and no one else has to see the bed. It'll get messy again soon anyway.

> *"Shoulding"*

"You should do this, you should do that."

When you use "should" you are telling your child that what doing just don't measure up to your expectations. This not only deals a blow to their self-esteem, but also reinforces ingrained perfectionism.

If you need to discipline your child, always end with a affection, such as a hug or kiss.

> *Quick Correction*

A child is very sensitive to criticism due to his ingrained strive for perfection and need to match up the adults' expectations.

If your child has difficulty reading a word, give him some time to try to sound it out. Your good intentions may be misinterpreted as a form of criticism. Parents should offer help and encourage your child to ask for assistance when needed.

> *Hiding your Mistakes*

Every child looks up to their parents as role models. If you are a perfectionist yourself, your child will see that in you and expect to model the same behavior - flawless.

The best thing you can do for your child as a parent is to admit your mistakes. Adults make mistakes too. Apologize if you have done something wrong, such as a spill, or if you accidentally bumped into him. Ask your child to forgive you, and most importantly, forgive yourself and let it go

Another way to show that you too are human and not as flawless, is to ask for help. Ask for help in deciding what to have for dinner (but provide the choices), or ask your child to do a simple task such as wiping the table.

> *Over-Relating*

If you have been a middle child and have gone through life feeling stuck in the middle, you will tend to sympathize with the feelings of your middle child. If you are a first born yourself, you are also going to sympathize with the perfectionistic strive your first-born child will have. The problem occurs when you overlook and reason a misbehavior with "I felt this way when I was his age."

Learn to differentiate between the matter itself and from personal experiences. This is especially important if you have to discipline more than one child for the same behavior. It would not make sense to send the first born to the room, and spare the younger sibling punishment, just because you knew it started off with the first born. Know what the reality is, and deal with it justly.

VIII.
BE READY: A NEW BABY COMING HOME

A new baby in the family is always great news to couples who have committed to raising a family responsibly. Grandparents and friends as well get excited as everyone prepares for the latest addition to the family circle. Daddy gets the crib and playroom ready while Mom is totally engrossed with taking good care of herself and the baby in her tummy.

Everything seems great to all the members of the family, but if you already have a first-born around, all the attention being directed to the arrival of a new baby can often leave the older sibling feeling neglected and detached. Especially when your first born is between 3 and 9 years old, do take extra care in making the child feel important and loved during these times.

Little children often think that a new baby will replace them to become the new favorite of the family. They see all the attention focused on the coming baby, and they begin to fear that they are no longer important. So, to get back the attention that seemed lost, an older child may create unusual, disruptive behavior to catch the attention of all those around him. Most often, the kid will begin to whine about little things that previously did not really matter. Others misbehave or bully other children in school, directing his suppressed anger to other children around him.

But it doesn't have to be this way. Parents can prevent feelings of insecurity in the older child so he will not get to hate the new baby. First, both parents should talk to the child about their plans of building the family, and the fun of having siblings around. Parents can lead the child to visualize the advantages of having siblings in the family. Simple examples such as having a seesaw partner or a playmate, not having to sleep alone in the dark, and all other occasions where two are better than one - help the child to picture it all out.

Get the older child involved in the preparations. Let them help clean the nursery and praise them for good deeds. Make them feel important in the whole preparation process. Keep to your usual routine with the child. If you read to your child at bedtime, don't stop doing it. Tell the child stories about how it was when they were in Mommy's tummy. If it is possible, always involve the older child.

IX.
NEW JOB OPPORTUNITY: MAKE A GOOD IMPRESSION

The recruitment process can be tough - you have to prove yourself throughout each stage - so once you've secured the job and got a fixed start date, it's important to make the best possible impression on your first day.

The first step to making a good impression comes a few days before your starting date - take time to learn about the company, their history, and their culture. It will help you to feel part of the organization - knowledge is power after all - and will show your employers that you really care about their business.

Secondly, be punctual. Showing up late creates an awful first impression, and you will probably be in a bit of a state, having hurried to get there on time. If you are driving, do a couple of practice runs in the days before, and be sure to leave a little earlier on your first morning. For users of public transport, be sure to fully research your route, and plan a back-up option in case your train or bus is cancelled or delayed.

It's always difficult knowing what to wear on your first day - take your cue from your interview, and the way your potential employers were dressed. Luckily some people are interviewed within the office in which they'll be working - if this is the case, take in your surroundings, as this can provide a fairly obvious idea of what is and isn't an acceptable attire.

When you arrive on time, dressed appropriately, walk in with confidence and a smile. Make eye contact, introduce yourself and be very polite. If you don't understand anything, ask questions - it may seem annoying but your employers would rather you ask instead of making a mistake or worry because you find something confusing.

Lastly, relax and enjoy the experience. It may seem daunting but if you follow these tips, you should have a successful and rewarding day - and remember that every single person at the company has had a first day, so they will understand how you feel and hopefully try to accommodate it in every way they can.

X.
A NEW BUSINESS: BE AWARE OF COMMON MISTAKES

We all work hard and dream of that day; we sweat, and work our minds and our hands to the bone. We have sacrificed and so have our family members—all for the promise of a highly successful business. Our hope is that our business will take us from where we are to the land of our dreams.

Then the day before we start our business comes, and we find ourselves feverishly working on the final details, making calls, sending emails etc. Maybe we are announcing a seminar registration to start at a specific time; we have sent the last-minute notices and now it's time for bed.

We lay there restlessly napping and then dawn finally arrives. We are now business owners, responsible for our own success. Sink or swim; it's up to us. what then can usually goes wrong for new business owners and more importantly what can we do to save face and profits?

The five most common mistakes made on the first day you start your business are;

> *Miscommunication*

This is a very common mistake in any business at any time, including the first day. Maybe you found out that your email or advertisement included the wrong date or time - yikes!!! So how can you recover from this mishap?

> *Delivery*

This is another very common mistake, don't depend on any one-time deliveries on your first day. For example; if you're going to have a book signing on your first day, do not rely on the delivery of your books on the day of your signing. Don't laugh, dozens of business owners do it all the time. Don't let it happen to you.

> ### ➢ *Weather*

This is also a common problem on your first day. Especially if you're doing business outside. Or maybe you're giving a seminar and you get some heavy snow, delaying or even preventing people from attending. This has happened more often than you might imagine.

> ### ➢ *Capacity*

If this happens in any way it can spell failure on day one, you could have way too many people show up, or not enough. Either way, it can lead to a massive failure.

> ### ➢ *Expectations*

This is the most common mistake on day one. Every business owner face this in some ways on day one. We either plan for too much business or not enough, or get ourselves worked up into a debilitating frenzy. Worrying, or even blindly investing and committing because we have unrealistic expectations.

So, what can we do to prevent this mistakes from happening on day one? Simply follow this formula, collect multiple ways to contact your clients, members or customers. Plan months ahead and do not rely on last minute deliveries or changes. Create a back-up plan for a bad weather day, maybe an alternate day if there is a weather delay. Plan for unexpected capacity, do some surveys and develop a realistic plan to handle your capacity, and follow that with realistic expectations based on facts.

CONCLUSION

"Be Inspired! Today is the first day of the rest of your life."

You can truly enjoy and look forward to the manifestations of your desires and dreams!

- April L. Thomas, MSW

www.ingramcontent.com/pod-product-compliance
Lightning Source LLC
Chambersburg PA
CBHW031531040426
42445CB00009B/482